Reading
Shakespeare
Today

ROMEO
and JULIET

Katie Griffiths

Cavendish
Square

New York

Published in 2016 by Cavendish Square Publishing, LLC
243 5th Avenue, Suite 136, New York, NY 10016

Copyright © 2016 by Cavendish Square Publishing, LLC

First Edition

Website: cavendishsq.com

This publication represents the opinions and views of the author based on his or her personal experience, knowledge, and
research. The information in this book serves as a general guide only. The author and publisher have used their best efforts in
preparing this book and disclaim liability rising directly or indirectly from the use and application of this book.

CPSIA Compliance Information: Batch #CW16CSQ

All websites were available and accurate when this book was sent to press.

Cataloging-in-Publication Data

Griffiths, Katie.
Romeo & Juliet / by Katie Griffiths.
p. cm. — (Reading Shakespeare today)
Includes index.
ISBN 978-1-5026-1036-2 (hardcover) ISBN 978-1-5026-1040-9 (ebook)
1. Shakespeare, William, 1564 - 1616. Romeo and Juliet — Juvenile literature. I. Griffiths, Katie. II. Title.
PR2831.G75 2016
822.3'3—d23

Editorial Director: David McNamara
Editor: Andrew Coddington
Copy Editor: Rebecca Rohan
Art Director: Jeffrey Talbot
Designer: Stephanie Flecha
Senior Production Manager: Jennifer Ryder-Talbot
Production Editor: Renni Johnson
Photo Research: J8 Media

The photographs in this book are used by permission and through the courtesy of: Mlenny Photography/Vetta/Getty Images,
cover and 1; (inkwell) Shutterstock.com, cover and chapter openers; (texture) Shutterstock.com, front, back cover and
throughout the book; Vvoronov/Shutterstock.com, 5; Nicholas Hilliard (1547-1619) [Public Domain] File: Elizabeth1 Phoenix.
jpg/Wikimedia Commons, 6; Padmayogini/Shutterstock.com, 9; Hank Walker/The LIFE Picture Collection/Getty Images,
11; Pictures from History/Bridgeman Images, 12; Georgios Kefalas/KEYSTONE/AP Images, 16; Sir John Gilbert, before
1873[Public Domain]/File: Act I-Scene 2.jpg/Wikimedia Commons, 18; © Moviestore Collection Ltd/Alamy, 21, 30, 38, 48;
Private Collection/Photo © The Fine Art Society, London, UK /Bridgeman Images, 23; 20th Century-Fox/Getty Images, 25;
Silver Screen Collection/Getty Images, 27; Ron/BHE Productions/Mary Evans Picture Library Ltd./age fotostock, 32; © Phillip
Jackson/Associated Newspapers/Daily Mail/Rex/Alamy, 35; Scott Barbour/Getty Images, 37; © Vibrant Pictures/Alamy, 41;
Sasha/Getty Images, 43; William James Grant (1829-66) / Shipley Art Gallery, Gateshead, Tyne & Wear, UK / © Tyne & Wear
Archives & Museums/Bridgeman Images 51; © Danilo Moroni/Alamy, 55; File: Frederic Leighton - The feigned death of Juliet -
Google Art Project.jpg [Public domain] via Wikimedia Commons, 57; Culture Club/Getty Images, 59; PARAMOUNT PICTURES/
Album/Newscom, 62; Bodo Marks/© dpa picture alliance/Alamy, 68; Fred Fehl/File: The Rumble from West Side Story 1957.
JPG/[Public domain], via Wikimedia Commons, 69; Ford Madox Brown (1821-1893) File: Romeo and Juliet Brown.jpg/Public
domain], via Wikimedia Commons, 74; Sir John Gilbert, before 1873[Public Domain]/File: Act I-Scene-1.jpg/via Wikimedia
Commons, 75; Leemage/Universal Images Group/Getty Images, 81.

Printed in the United States of America

CONTENTS

Introduction   **4**
Shakespeare and His World

Chapter 1   **8**
Shakespeare and *Romeo and Juliet*

Chapter 2   **14**
The Play's the Thing

Chapter 3   **73**
A Closer Look

Chronology   **94**

A Shakespeare Glossary   **96**

Suggested Essay Topics   **102**

Test Your Memory   **103**

Further Information   **106**

Bibliography   **109**

Index   **110**

About the Author   **112**

Introduction

SHAKESPEARE AND HIS WORLD

Romeo and Juliet may be the most famous love story of all time. This tale of doomed love has inspired hundreds of writers and readers, while people from all over the world use Shakespeare's words to express their own hopes and fears. But who is Shakespeare? And why do his characters continue to speak to us through the centuries?

Very little is known about the life of William Shakespeare. During his lifetime, information was often poorly kept or not recorded at all. All we have is a few facts and our own imagination. Shakespeare was born in Stratford-upon-Avon, a town in Warwickshire, England, in April 1564. He was one of several children born to John and Mary Shakespeare, though most of his siblings died young. His father was a glove maker, often in trouble with the law, though this was most likely due to his lack of church attendance, which was seen as a political act during this period. In 1582, when Shakespeare was eighteen, he married Anne Hathaway, who was eight years his senior. He first rose to fame in 1593 with a long poem titled _Venus and Adonis_.

Shakespeare was born a few years into the reign of Queen Elizabeth I. She would eventually become the

Illustration of William Shakespeare

Queen Elizabeth I of England

last Tudor monarch, and during their dynasty her family completely changed the face of England. Her father, in order to divorce Elizabeth's mother, had broken from the Catholic Church and established his own branch of Christianity in England. It was known as the Church of England, and the King, not the Pope, was its head. This action threw the country into civil war, pitting Catholics against Protestants (followers of the new Church of England). When Elizabeth's half-sister Mary took the throne, she used her power to try and return the country to Catholicism, burning and torturing hundreds of Protestants. By the time Elizabeth came to power, the country was exhausted and racked by religious conflict. She brought a tentative peace through her decision to uphold her father's new Church—realizing that her sister's zeal had not brought about a more unified England.

Shakespeare's plays often echo this political tension and fear of a return of chaos. Sometimes he directly addresses the audience's fears, and sometimes he provides an escape from England's harsh realities, creating characters who are often trying to escape reality themselves. *Romeo and Juliet* walks a fine line between both these concepts. Verona is a city experiencing its own civil war, with two large wealthy families breaking the peace and piling bodies up in the streets. Romeo and Juliet are two teenagers trying to forget about their families' atrocities by losing themselves in the fantasy of their love. Read bleakly, *Romeo and Juliet* shows us how hard realities can crush dreams; but read hopefully, we can argue that it shows the need for fantasy in order to cure a sick society.

Chapter One

Shakespeare and *Romeo and Juliet*

omeo and Juliet is one of Shakespeare's early plays. It was first performed in 1594–1595 when London playhouses reopened after an outbreak of the plague. Ten thousand people died of the disease in London alone. Shakespeare alludes to it in the play when a message is not delivered because of the plague. At the first performance, Romeo was played by leading actor Richard Burbage, and Juliet by Master Robert Goffe. Women could not legally appear on stage until the late seventeenth century, so female parts were played by boys.

Like all great writers, William Shakespeare wrote about things he knew. A major example is the role of Juliet. A Queen may have ruled Elizabethan England, but female

Performers at the Globe Theatre in London

power largely began and ended with her. There was a great difference in lifestyle between men and women. As a young woman, Juliet had no power or choice in society. Her life was controlled by men, first her father and then, presumably, the man her father chose to be her husband. In this case, she defied convention by secretly marrying Romeo. However, the fact that her father could—and did—arrange her marriage to Paris shows the power that men held. It also sealed Juliet's fate.

Social structure was tight and fixed in Elizabethan society. In Verona, Peter, servant to the Capulets, is poorly educated and cannot read, so he has no power either. His illiteracy and his status bind him forever within the

Love and Rebels

IN *ROMEO AND JULIET*, there is no room for weak emotion. Love is all-powerful and life altering. Hate is all-consuming. Within this play, we see some of arguably the greatest love dialogue ever written.

It is not hard to see the attraction of these emotions. Romeo and Juliet feel wonderful things for each other. Their emotions are so great that they are willing to suffer and suffer again in order to hold on to the feeling. They will sacrifice everything for another person that, even by the end of the play, they have only known a total of four days. In fact, so great is their passion that the play has become synonymous with forbidden love. Romeo and Juliet types have cropped up in many different corners of culture, from movies and TV shows to books and even other plays.

Despite Shakespeare's clear love and respect for his characters, the violence of their lives and deaths might make an audience question his admiration for young love that rebels against society. Most of Shakespeare's comedies and love stories end in marriage. For Shakespeare, the best way to reward a good character was a love match and a wedding. Yet, within *Romeo and Juliet*, the wedding is not a happy moment of completion, but the tipping point that sends the tragic hand of fate working overtime. In a strange way, the lovers have not yet earned their happy ending. To create a lasting marriage, they must first repair the society that prevents it. But this is an awful lot of responsibility for two teenagers, and even the play's opening monologue makes it clear that nothing but their deaths will end the feud. The unfairness of this situation and the ironic cruelty strikes a universal chord in all readers.

Tony and Maria in *West Side Story*

Majnun and Layla, the Arabian versions of Romeo and Juliet

social structure. That rigid structure weaves through and influences the play's events.

Romeo and Juliet is often called the ultimate love story, but it is as much about hate as it is about love. Besides a tragic marriage, it tells of two families and the deadly feud that rules their lives and those of the people who surround them.

Shakespeare did not make up the story of Romeo and Juliet. Nor did he introduce the theme to theater audiences. It was already a popular tale in European folklore and had been translated into an English poem called *The Tragicall Historye of Romeus and Juliet*. Shakespeare embellished the old story and adapted it for the stage. He contrasted the innocence of the young lovers with the crude sexuality of other characters. He shortened the time frame from months to just four days. That allowed just a single night for the lovers to spend together. In the poem, Romeo kills Tybalt in self-defense. However, Shakespeare has Tybalt kill Mercutio, which drives Romeo to fight and kill him. Shakespeare also changed Juliet's age from sixteen to thirteen to make her appear more vulnerable. He makes her father move the wedding day ahead from Thursday to Wednesday. These and other changes emphasize speed, and how quickly the young couple become involved. This urgency creates the intense pressure that inevitably leads to tragedy and death.

Though the story of *Romeo and Juliet* was not new, Shakespeare's skill brought out the individuality of his characters, distinguishing him from most other artists of his time and since. He took a theme that was already known and created what is now regarded as the greatest love story of all time.

Chapter Two

The Play's the Thing

Act I, Prologue

Overview

The Chorus (presented as one character) enters and describes the noble Capulet and Montague families in a sonnet:

> *Two households, both alike in dignity,*
> *In fair Verona, where we lay our scene,*

The ancient grudge between them has become violent:

> *From ancient grudge break to new mutiny,*
> *Where civil blood makes civil hands unclean.*

Romeo and Juliet are described as victims of fate:

> *From forth the fatal loins of these two foes*
> *A pair of star-crossed lovers take their life;*

And there is no mistaking the outcome of this tragedy:

> *Whole misadventured piteous overthrows*
> *Do with their death bury their parents' strife*

Analysis

The Chorus not only sets the scene, but also tells the audience exactly what will happen. The phrase *star-crossed* is used because, at that time, stars were thought to control human destiny. The lack of suspense about the outcome emphasizes a major theme of the tragedy—fate. From the very beginning, the audience realizes that the lovers will die. Death is their fate. There is no escape.

Act I, Scene 1

Overview

Two Capulet servants, Sampson and Gregory, engage in loud, boastful, and vulgar conversation, most of which concerns the character of Montague men and women and what members of the Capulet household will do to them. When servants of the Montague household enter, they are immediately drawn into a street brawl. One of the Montagues, Benvolio, Romeo's cousin, comes upon this conflict. A peacemaker (his name means "goodwill"), Benvolio draws his sword in an attempt to stop the fighting. At that moment, the fiery Capulet kinsman Tybalt enters. When he sees Benvolio's drawn sword, he needs no other excuse to attack. The brawl widens as more citizens become involved.

At this point, the heads of the two feuding households, Montague and Capulet, arrive with their wives. Instead

The Royal Swedish Ballet performs *Romeo and Juliet*.

of calming the scene, they go to attack one another, but their wives intervene. Prince Escalus, who is in charge of law and order in Verona, enters and orders everyone to stop the fighting. He declares that the feud has gone on for too long and must stop. He pronounces a death sentence for anyone who further disturbs the peace.

Everyone now disperses except for Montague, Lady Montague, and their nephew Benvolio. The Montagues are worried about their son Romeo, who seems melancholy lately. Benvolio promises to find out what troubles the young man. The parents leave, and a depressed Romeo enters. He tells Benvolio he is in love with a beautiful young woman named Rosaline, but she spurns him. Benvolio urges Romeo to forget Rosaline, but Romeo says he cannot.

Analysis

The opening street brawl introduces all of the players of Verona's society that are important to the play. It also stresses an important concept in Elizabethan England and this play: masculine honor. No matter the consequences, a man of Verona—whether he is a servant or noble—must defend his honor against any transgression. How easily this concept leads to trouble is seen in the characters of peacemaker Benvolio and hot-tempered Tybalt. Benvolio draws his sword hoping to make the troublemakers back down. Tybalt sees the sword as an invitation to fight.

Romeo, the protagonist and lover, enters at the end of the scene. It is here that the focus switches from hate to love. Expecting talk of Romeo's love for Juliet, the audience is shocked to find out that he is in love with Rosaline. At this early point in the play, Romeo is shown as a young man more in love with the idea of love than with an actual person. He even speaks in a youthful manner, which changes to more mature verse as he falls in love with Juliet. Romeo also speaks of love in military terms, stressing Shakespeare's idea of how close love and hate are.

Act I, Scene 2

Overview

Capulet is engaged in conversation with Count Paris, who wishes to marry Juliet. Capulet is pleased, for he knows

The Capulet servant struggles to read the invite list.

that Paris is a kinsman of Prince Escalus. Yet, acting as a father, Capulet tells Paris that Juliet is too young to marry. The marriage must be postponed for two years. However, to indicate that he is in favor of the union, Capulet invites Paris to a masquerade that evening. That way, Paris can get to know Juliet and win her affection. Capulet calls his servant Peter, giving him a list of people to invite to the feast. The two men leave, and Peter is left alone. He worries because he cannot read the names on the list.

When Romeo and Benvolio stroll by, Peter asks Romeo to read the list to him. Romeo sees that Rosaline is on the list. Assuming they are not Montagues, Peter invites them to the masquerade. Romeo accepts, thinking to see Rosaline there. Benvolio goes along with this, believing that the sight of other beautiful women will distract Romeo from his infatuation with Rosaline.

Analysis

Count Paris is introduced as Capulet's choice of a husband for Juliet. In addition, the audience learns that Romeo and Juliet are going to meet, and the expectations are that the young man's feelings about Rosaline are going to change. Through the conversation between Paris and Capulet, Juliet's social status is established. As a young woman in Verona, she has almost no say concerning her future. Although Capulet appears to want what is best for his daughter, Paris's position as a relative of the prince is obviously of greater importance than Juliet's happiness. Capulet speaks of his daughter's youth and innocence. That may indicate parental concern; it may also be thrown out as an enticement for Paris. Although Capulet insists that the marriage must wait two years, he immediately invites Paris to the feast so that he might begin to court Juliet.

The audience realizes even at this early stage that circumstances have already sealed Romeo and Juliet's fate before they meet. The two unknowing rivals are contrasted: Paris, the courteous, well-to-do suitor, and Romeo, the idealistic youth who is in love with love. The servant Peter provides humor but indicates that the poor and illiterate also have very little power.

Act I, Scene 3

Overview

Prior to the masquerade, Lady Capulet asks the Nurse to find her daughter. The Nurse is Juliet's nanny. Once Juliet arrives, Lady Capulet sends the Nurse away, but quickly changes her mind and asks her to stay to give whatever counsel she can in the conversation. However, the Nurse begins a long story linking Juliet as an innocent bystander to a sexual joke. In effect, an incident where she fell on her back as a toddler inspired a lewd comment made by the Nurse's husband that Juliet will do so again with a sexual partner when she is grown. Juliet is embarrassed, but Lady Capulet cannot get the Nurse to stop talking. Finally, when the Nurse mentions marriage, Lady Capulet says that is what she wished to discuss with her daughter. She asks Juliet if she has given any thought to marriage. Juliet says it is an honor that she has not considered. When her mother says that Paris is interested in her, Juliet dutifully replies that she will talk to him at the feast.

Analysis

This is our first look at the other title character. Juliet's lack of power over her own life is emphasized. Her mother, who also married at a young age, agrees with her husband that Paris is a good prospect for Juliet. The Nurse is shown as a comic character; her coarse outlook on life is contrasted with Juliet's innocence. Her joke indicates that, since birth, Juliet has been viewed as a potential sexual partner for her husband.

The relationship between mother and daughter is clear. Lady Capulet is cold and distant. She wants only for

Natasha Parry, Olivia Hussey, and Pat Heywood in the 1968 film of the play

Juliet to obey her father's wishes, with which she concurs. She, too, sees the union with Paris as a social boon for the family and makes no attempt to consider her daughter's feelings in the matter. She regards marriage as a way to increase wealth, and the Nurse regards marriage as nothing more than a sexual act. Neither woman can understand a romantic concept of love.

Juliet is clearly not in favor of an arranged marriage. The young girl cleverly replies that she will meet him and see what she thinks: "I'll look to like, if looking liking move / But no more deep will I endart my eye. ..." Young and innocent as she is, Juliet's answer indicates her growing emotional maturity. She has no intention of marrying someone she does not love. Although Juliet's innocence is stressed, an inner strength appears. Her evasive answer to her mother will blossom later into open defiance against her parents.

Act I, Scene 4

Overview

Wearing masks, Romeo, Benvolio, and their friend Mercutio join other masked guests on their way to the Capulets' house. Romeo worries that, as Montagues, they will not be allowed to enter. His friends laugh at that concern. The still-melancholy Romeo says that, even if they are allowed in, he will not dance. Mercutio mocks him, turning all of Romeo's statements of love into sexual references. Finally Mercutio launches into the tale of Queen Mab of the fairies and becomes quite passionate in his delivery. Romeo steps in and calms him down. As the three continue to the hall, Romeo voices concern about the night's activities, fearing that they might eventually lead to death. However, with his friends around him, he shrugs off his fears and continues to the feast.

Analysis

The clever and witty Mercutio is introduced in this scene. His Queen Mab speech is one of the play's most famous.

Queen Mab

He talks of the fairy queen who gives people dreams as she rides through the night. But the dreams she brings are nightmares, fortifying whatever vice the sleeper has, such as lust or violence. In his highly nonsensical but colorful speech, Mercutio suggests that desires like Romeo's are as silly and fragile as the fairy queen. Such a suggestion is in sharp contrast to both Romeo and Juliet, who view true love as a noble condition. Mercutio proves himself to be a master of puns. He is also shown as the friend who can jest with Romeo as no one else can. He is down-to-earth, unlike Romeo the daydreamer. His energetic character is established, not only as a foil to Romeo's seriousness, but also so that the audience will have sympathy for him when he is later killed.

This scene does not move the plot forward, since the audience already knows that Romeo and his friends are going to the feast. The audience also already knows that Romeo will suffer an untimely death, but his references to death point to the general sense of fate taking over. In fact, his final speech in the scene indicates impending doom, which casts a shadow on the feast itself.

In this scene, for the first time, the audience becomes aware of a tragic tone. *Romeo and Juliet* is often spoken of as a great tragedy. But when one first reads *Romeo and Juliet*, it does not seem like a tragedy. Although the play opens with a brawl, the fighters are almost comical characters, fighting over trivial nonsense. It all ends peacefully after the prince sends them home. The rest of the scene concerns Romeo's melancholy over the indifferent Rosaline. This may be sad for Romeo, but it is still not a tragedy. But in Scene 4, the audience senses that tragedy will follow.

Act I, Scene 5

Overview

The scene opens in the Capulets' house, with the masked ball in full swing. Capulet interacts with his guests, particularly his nephew Tybalt. Romeo enters and sees Juliet across the room. He asks a servant to identify her, but the servant replies that he does not know her name. From that moment on, Rosaline no longer exists, and Romeo knows that he has never been in love until this moment. As he speaks aloud of his feelings, Tybalt recognizes Romeo's voice. Tybalt knows that Romeo is a Montague and calls for a

Claire Danes and Leonardo DiCaprio in *Romeo + Juliet* (1996)

servant to bring him his sword. He intends to fight this intruder. But Capulet intervenes, saying that Romeo has a good reputation in Verona, and Capulet will not have any bloodshed at his feast. He makes Tybalt agree not to cause trouble. Although he feels his honor has been slighted, Tybalt obeys his uncle but secretly vows to get revenge on Romeo.

Romeo crosses the room and boldly approaches Juliet. In the first four lines of his sonnet, he describes himself as a pilgrim who needs her saintly kiss to absolve him of sin. Juliet responds by continuing the sonnet, then quietly allows the kiss. Then she asks if her lips now contain his sin since they have kissed. Romeo wants his sin back, so they kiss again. At this point, the Nurse appears and tells Juliet that her mother wants her. Romeo asks the Nurse who Juliet is and is devastated to learn that she is a Capulet. Benvolio arrives to take Romeo home.

Now Juliet asks the Nurse to learn Romeo's identity. She fears she will die if she finds out that he is married. Instead, she is appalled to discover that she has fallen in love with a Montague. Following the Nurse, she leaves the hall.

Analysis

The first meeting of the lovers takes over the scene. Delaying their first meeting until the end of Act I is well justified by the poetic language, which creates wonder and excitement. Struck by her beauty, Romeo engages Juliet in a conversation that is tinged with religion. It indicates that their love will become associated with divine purity. Before their first kiss, Romeo and Juliet speak in sonnet form, which Shakespeare uses to express their perfect love. Romeo indicates that he can now tell the difference between his anguish over Rosaline and what he is experiencing at this moment: "I ne'er saw true beauty till this night." He is changing before the audience's eyes from a young boy in love with love to a man who has caught the beginnings of true passion.

In the first kiss, Romeo is the initiator, but Juliet uses language that encourages the second kiss. With that short exchange, the innocent young girl becomes one who understands what she wants. This sense of immediate rapture between the two is emphasized by the fact that neither Romeo nor Juliet thinks to ask the other's name.

Michael York as Tybalt in *Romeo and Juliet* (1968)

In spite of the initial wonder, the scene carries a mood of impending tragedy, which the audience immediately recognizes. Tybalt endures what he feels is an insult. The audience realizes that there will be trouble between him and Romeo. Tybalt will at some point ignore his uncle's wish to leave Romeo alone, showing that this feud extends not just to the heads of the households but throughout the families and across generations.

Even before Juliet learns Romeo's identity, she says she would die if she cannot marry him. The image that identifies death as Juliet's bridegroom occurs often during the play. This first meeting between the star-crossed lovers is the first step toward their deaths.

Act II, Prologue

Overview

The Chorus enters with another sonnet, which expresses how Romeo and Juliet feel after meeting:

> *Now Romeo is beloved and loves again,*
> *Alike bewitched by the charm of looks*

and the troubles they will suffer because of their two families:

> *Being held a foe, he may not have access*
> *To breathe such vows as lovers use to swear.*

Analysis

The prologue helps build suspense, stressing the problems that the lovers face. It also contrasts Romeo's rejected love for Rosaline and the mutual passion that is immediately evident with Juliet.

Act II, Scene 1

After leaving the feast, Romeo decides he must find Juliet. He enters the Capulet property and leaps over a wall into the orchard. Mercutio and Benvolio search for him. They are sure he is nearby. Amused and somewhat annoyed, Mercutio launches into a rather obscene and mocking speech about Romeo and Rosaline. Romeo hears the speech but does not want to be found, so he does not respond. Then Mercutio and Benvolio leave.

Analysis

This scene contrasts Mercutio's understanding of love as a physical conquest and the sense that Romeo has moved beyond that in his feeling for Juliet. His leap over the wall signifies this change. He has moved beyond his friend. In addition, Romeo's leap over the wall signifies that he is separating from friends and family in order to be with Juliet.

Act II, Scene 2

Overview

With Romeo silent in the orchard, Juliet appears at her window in the Capulet house. He does not speak to her but compares her to the morning sun, far more beautiful than the moon it takes away. Not aware of his presence, Juliet speaks aloud about the fate that has placed her and Romeo in two warring families. She bemoans their names, saying that she would refuse her name if he said he loved her. At this point, Romeo answers her, but she is afraid that he will be killed if he is discovered.

Olivia Hussey and Leonard Whiting in *Romeo and Juliet* (1968)

The two speak of love, with Juliet growing afraid that they have found this passion too quickly. Romeo reassures her that their love is real. She disappears and reappears at the window as the Nurse repeatedly calls to her. Finally Juliet appears and tells Romeo that a messenger will seek him out the following day to confirm Romeo's intention to wed her. Juliet goes into her chamber, and Romeo departs.

Analysis

In what is one of the most famous scenes in theater, the romance of young love dominates the action. This is also the happiest and least tragic scene of the play, filled with lovely poetic images. In his passion, Romeo describes Juliet as the sun, meaning that their love moves him into spiritual light. Yet it is obvious that their circumstances dictate that they must meet in darkness.

Romeo begins to mature in this scene, indicated by the fact that he speaks more in blank verse than in rhymes as he used earlier. Yet Juliet remains the more mature of the two. It is she who mentions marriage, for instance, and makes the arrangements for a meeting the next day. Her reference to the family names points out a major conflict, the feud that will lead to their deaths. Her comings and goings from the window heighten the tension and speed up the action. In addition, Juliet tells Romeo:

> *And all my fortunes at thy foot I'll lay*
> *And follow thee, my lord, throughout the world.*

It is an ironic promise, since she will follow him into death.

Act II, Scene 3

Overview

In the early morning, Friar Lawrence has been collecting herbs and flowers from his garden. He speaks of the benefits of these plants, showing knowledge of their properties. When Romeo enters, the Friar senses that the young man has been out all night and fears that he has slept with Rosaline, which the Friar would consider a sin. Instead Romeo reveals he is passionately in love with Juliet and wants to marry her. This shocks the Friar because of its suddenness. He comments that young love is fickle, but Romeo protests. He tells the Friar that his love is true and

Leonard Whiting and Milo O'Shea as Romeo and Friar Lawrence

that Juliet feels the same way. The Friar is not convinced. However, he does agree to perform their marriage ceremony, hoping this will end the brutal and senseless feud between the two families.

Analysis

This introduction of the Friar highlights the tension between good and evil. He wants to end the feud. That is why he agrees to help the lovers get married. The Friar is also an expert on medicinal plants. He speaks knowingly of their healing and harming powers. This dual nature of plants suggests that good and evil live together in both nature and people. The pull between good and evil is constant throughout the play. The Friar himself is a good example of a man with conflicting characteristics. His heart is in the right place, but his method of marrying the young couple without their families' knowledge will lead to tragedy for both families.

Friar Lawrence is both a confidant and a father figure to Romeo. The relationship between the two highlights the theme of youth versus age. Romeo tells no one except the Friar about his feelings for Juliet, highlighting his growing isolation. As a young man in love, Romeo is eager to get married. He wants the Friar to marry him and Juliet that very day. But the Friar, not convinced of Romeo's true feelings, advises restraint.

Act II, Scene 4

Overview

On a street in Verona, Mercutio wonders aloud where Romeo spent the previous night because he did not return home. Benvolio says that Tybalt has sent a letter to the Montague household. Still suffering "insult" of Romeo's attendance at the Capulet feast, Tybalt has challenged Romeo to a duel. Mercutio jokes that Romeo is already dead because he has been struck by Cupid's arrow. When

Romeo arrives, Mercutio continues his teasing. The two young men carry on some sexual verbal jousting.

The Nurse and Peter arrive looking for Romeo. Mercutio teases the Nurse, calling her a harlot, or prostitute. After Mercutio and Benvolio leave, the Nurse warns Romeo that he must not fool with Juliet's feelings. He declares that he will not. He says they will be married that afternoon if the Nurse can get Juliet to the Friar's cell. The Nurse agrees and also agrees to receive a rope ladder from a Montague servant so that Romeo can spend their wedding night in Juliet's chamber.

Analysis

The sexual banter between Romeo and Mercutio contrasts with the impending disaster noted in Tybalt's challenge. Tybalt is quick-tempered and vengeful. Romeo, once melancholy, is now above this. He thinks only of his all-consuming love. His elation is such that he can answer Mercutio's barbed remarks with equally lively retorts. Mercutio's comments are ironic, since he still believes Romeo is passionate about Rosaline.

Mercutio's quick-tempered nature comes forth in this scene. He shows a growing antagonism for Tybalt and scorns Tybalt's challenge. The urgency is increased, as is the emphasis between love and hate. Tybalt is always ready for a fight, and he has made it his mission to carry on the hostility between the families. Romeo, on the other hand, has risen above such concerns in his love for Juliet.

There are many references to time throughout this scene. Time plays a very important role. The period from

Mercutio teases the Nurse in the square.

when the lovers meet at the feast until their wedding night covers just twenty-four hours.

Act II, Scene 5

Overview

Juliet has been waiting impatiently for the Nurse to return with news of Romeo. Finally the Nurse arrives. She teases that she is too out of breath to tell Juliet the news. But she relents and says that Juliet is to meet Romeo at the Friar's, where they will be married. Meanwhile, the Nurse is to await Romeo's servant, who is bringing the ladder so Romeo can enter Juliet's chamber that night.

Analysis

The speed of the events in the preceding scene contrasts with the hours that Juliet waited to hear the news. This scene is all about the wonder and the elation of romantic love. Both lovers are filled with anticipation. Unlike in the previous scenes, Juliet acts more like the thirteen-year-old that she is. This also contrasts with the slow movements of the Nurse. She makes Juliet frantic with her deliberate and slow tale before she reveals what Romeo said. Like Mercutio's, the Nurse's view is that love is no more than a physical relationship, and she also shares his bawdy sense of humor. She touches once again on life and death when she comments that Juliet will have pleasure on her wedding night, but hints that pregnancy will follow. The audience knows that Juliet will marry but will not live to bear children.

Jane McDonald and Lorna Want as the Nurse and Juliet in *Romeo and Juliet: The Musical*

Act II, Scene 6

Overview

Romeo waits in the Friar's cell for Juliet to arrive. He speaks of the joyful passion he feels, but the Friar cautions him to love more moderately. When Juliet arrives, Romeo showers her with romantic words. The Friar realizes that moderation will not work at this moment. He says, "Come, come with me, and we will make short work; / For, by

Romeo and Juliet wed.

your leaves, you shall not stay alone, / Till Holy Church incorporate two in one." Then the three exit to go to the wedding ceremony.

Analysis

Two things highlight the wedding scene. It is very brief, and for all rhetoric of love, there is a feeling of impending doom. The Friar speaks of Romeo and Juliet's passion, warning, "These violent delights have violent ends." He calls for moderation. Yet that is not the way that Romeo and Juliet, or any of the other characters, live their lives. The passion of the lovers is portrayed as beautiful, but in the end it will prove destructive. Romeo says, "Then love-devouring Death do what he dare— / It is enough I may but call her mine." He is saying that the happiness he feels in marrying Juliet cannot even be marred by death. His words foreshadow the fact that death will indeed be victorious over them both.

Act III, Scene 1

Overview

Later that afternoon, Benvolio, not wanting another brawl, tells Mercutio that perhaps they should go indoors because he is afraid they might meet Capulet kinsmen. Mercutio scorns that idea. Soon, Tybalt and his friends appear. Tybalt asks to speak to them, which annoys Mercutio, who starts to provoke him. When Romeo enters, Tybalt dares him to fight. But Romeo, who is now married to Juliet and therefore is kin to Tybalt, says that he does not wish to fight. He remarks that Tybalt will understand his refusal when he learns the reason for it. At this point Mercutio, who does not understand Romeo's reluctance to fight, becomes even more annoyed. He declares that he will fight Tybalt. Because Tybalt lets no remark go unchallenged, he draws his sword. Romeo tries to get between the two men, but Mercutio is stabbed. Tybalt and his men leave, and Mercutio exits to die, blaming both families: "A plague o' both your houses."

Romeo now despises himself for being cowardly and causing his friend's death:

> *This gentleman, the Prince's near ally*
> *My very friend, hath got this mortal hurt*
> *In my behalf; my reputation stained*
> *With Tybalt's slander—Tybalt, that an hour*
> *Hath been my cousin! O sweet Juliet,*
> *Thy beauty hath made me effeminate*
> *And in my temper softened valor's steel!*

Tybalt reenters, and Romeo draws his sword. Again, Tybalt responds. In the ensuing battle, Romeo kills Tybalt. Benvolio, seeing a crowd approaching, tells Romeo to flee, which he does.

A crowd appears, along with Prince Escalus and the Montagues and Capulets. Benvolio explains to the prince that Romeo tried to stop the initial fight between Tybalt and Mercutio. Lady Capulet, however, says that Benvolio is lying. She demands Romeo's death. Instead, the prince orders Romeo to be exiled from Verona. If he does not leave the city, he will be put to death.

Analysis

The sudden death of Mercutio assures the audience that the play will now take a tragic turn. The emphasis upon

The Rasta Thomas' Dance Company's adaptation of *Romeo and Juliet*

love in the previous scene switches dramatically to death and violence. It is obvious that what really matters in Verona is masculine honor. Impulsive Romeo becomes enraged at himself for letting his joy over marrying Juliet turn him into a "coward." The result is Mercutio's death. In the society of the time, it was generally believed that a man who was too much in love was unmanly. Romeo speaks of himself as "effeminate."

Ironically, Mercutio dies thinking his fatal injury stems from the feud between the two houses. He never finds out about Romeo's love for Juliet. Even more ironic is Romeo's attack on Tybalt, which results from his rage over Mercutio's death. By killing Tybalt in fury, Romeo acts the same way as the quick-tempered Tybalt and Mercutio. Another irony is that Romeo's refusal to fight Tybalt results in the very violence he tried to avoid. Throughout the scene, passion overcomes reason.

Act III, Scene 2

Overview

Juliet impatiently waits in the orchard, longing for darkness so that Romeo will join her for their wedding night. The Nurse appears with news of the duel between Romeo and Tybalt. The Nurse's jumble of hasty words leads Juliet to believe that Romeo is dead. The distraught Nurse tries to explain further. Now Juliet thinks that both Romeo and Tybalt have died. At last the Nurse calms down and explains. But when Juliet learns that Romeo has killed Tybalt and been exiled, she faults him for rashness. The Nurse quickly agrees, and she, too, criticizes Romeo. Now Juliet chides the Nurse and herself for criticizing Romeo. She moans aloud that there will be no wedding night. The Nurse, however, says she knows where Romeo is hiding and assures Juliet that he will come to her. Juliet gives the Nurse a ring to give to Romeo.

Analysis

The sense of impending doom is again evident in this scene. Juliet waits for night to arrive, expressing her frustration at the slow pace of the daylight hours. Meanwhile the audience already knows about the tragedy that has occurred. The differences between the Nurse and Juliet, and between age versus youth, are accented here. The Nurse blames Romeo because she views life without emotion. Romeo has killed a Capulet; therefore, Romeo must be punished. She cannot understand the depth of Juliet's love. Juliet, who initially feels conflicted, quickly realizes that her loyalty is to her husband. As Romeo is leaving his friends and family behind, so Juliet, too, is leaving the Capulets to share a life with her husband. She is emerging as a young woman with her own opinions and emotions. The split between Juliet and the Nurse widens as Juliet realizes that she can no longer count on the older woman for guidance. Shakespeare often

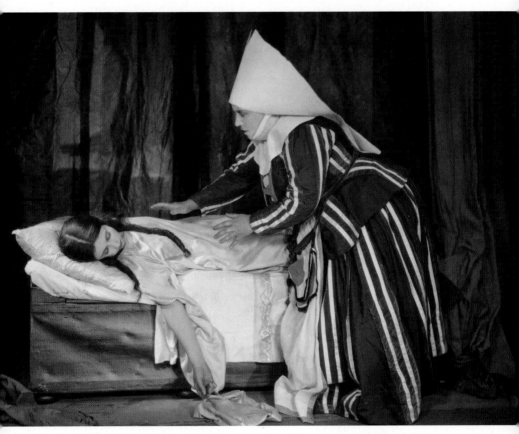

Gwen Ffrangcon-Davies and Barbara Gott at the Regent Theatre (1924)

links young love with suicide and death, and there is great psychological tension in this scene. When Juliet mistakenly believes Romeo is dead, she assumes that he killed himself and that she will do the same. Even when she knows that he is alive but has been banished, she equates banishment with doom. She says that she will go to her wedding bed, not with Romeo, but with death.

Light and dark images are important in creating the mood of this scene and foreshadowing. As Juliet waits for news, she views the approaching night with pleasure because Romeo will be with her. It is in darkness that they will share their love, and, as the audience knows, it is in darkness that they will enter eternity.

Act III, Scene 3

Overview

In the Friar's cell, Romeo waits for news of his fate. When the Friar enters and tells him that he is fortunate because the sentence is banishment, not death, Romeo is distraught. He says that the sentence is worse than death because he cannot live without Juliet. He ignores the Friar's attempts to comfort him and falls to the floor.

The Nurse enters. Thinking that Juliet now regards him as a murderer for killing her cousin, Romeo threatens to stab himself. The Friar chides him for being unmanly and offers a plan. Romeo will see Juliet that night, but he must leave her and Verona before dawn. He will stay in Mantua while the Friar spreads the news about their marriage. The Friar hopes such news will end the feud and unite the families. Romeo agrees, joyfully accepts Juliet's ring from the Nurse, and says good-bye to the Friar.

Analysis

The emotional differences between Romeo and Juliet are contrasted here. When Juliet thinks she has to live without Romeo, she is grief-stricken and bemoans her fate. When Romeo thinks he must live without Juliet, he tries to stab himself and end the suffering. Also, in his heightened emotional state, Romeo cannot accept the calm reasoning of the Friar. Again, there is the conflict between young and old. The Friar does not comprehend the depth of Romeo's passion, and that very passion prevents Romeo from following the rational advice that might have changed his fate.

Again the marriage of the lovers is linked to death. In the previous scene, Juliet likened Romeo's banishment to death. When he hears his punishment in this scene, Romeo, too, speaks of death. The Friar himself links the marriage to death: "Affliction is enamored of thy parts / And thou art wedded to calamity." But no matter how the Friar reasons with him, Romeo is too upset to accept the older man's assurances.

Act III, Scene 4

Overview

Capulet, Lady Capulet, and Paris meet after Tybalt's death. Capulet tells Paris that, despite the tragedy, his daughter will abide by his wishes for the marriage once she has finished grieving. Actually, no need to wait; he is certain she will do as he says. He and Paris arrange for the wedding to be held on Thursday. He tells his wife to go to Juliet before she retires and inform her of the impending marriage.

Analysis

The reason why Capulet decides that the wedding must take place so quickly is not explained. It might be that, with the recent added friction, it would be to Capulet's advantage to have Paris, a kinsman of the prince, on his side. Capulet later says that he wants happiness for his daughter. However, it is obvious that he and his wife want this marriage for social reasons and have no concern for Juliet's feelings. They would not understand a marriage based solely on love.

An impetuous man, Capulet earlier told Paris at the feast that Juliet will agree to the match. Now he declares that she will obey his wishes. Ironically, Juliet is already married to Romeo. The scene highlights the powerlessness of women in Verona. This is emphasized by the fact that Capulet had earlier declared that the marriage could not take place for two years. Now it will take place in a mere three days.

The many references to time in this scene speed up the action. They create a sense of urgency as the characters rush headlong to their inevitable fate. The tension between young and old, parents and children, is also noted. Capulet decides Juliet's future without consulting her.

Act III, Scene 5

Overview

It is nearly dawn in Juliet's chamber, and the lovers must part. Again, their love flourishes in darkness. Juliet passionately tries to prolong Romeo's exit. She tells him that the bird they hear is a nightingale, rather than the morning lark. She says that the light outside her chamber window is that of a meteor, not the sun.

Both lovers are well aware that if Romeo is found in Verona that morning, it will mean death. Nonetheless, Romeo listens to Juliet's pleas and declares that he will stay and face death rather than leave her. When she hears this, Juliet relents and says Romeo must go.

The Nurse enters to say that Lady Capulet is coming. The lovers part, and Romeo leaves from the balcony. As he does, Juliet looks down on him and thinks he looks pale, as though he were dead in the bottom of a tomb. Romeo says she also looks pale to him, but it is only their grief that makes them look so. He leaves, and Juliet responds to her mother's call.

Lady Capulet enters and thinks Juliet is tearful because of Tybalt. She tells her daughter that she wants Romeo dead. In a speech cleverly filled with puns, Juliet lets her mother think that she, too, wants Romeo dead, even while she is actually speaking of their love. But when Lady Capulet tells Juliet that her father has decided she will be married on Thursday, Juliet refuses.

Capulet enters and becomes enraged at Juliet's refusal, calling her "young baggage" and "disobedient wretch." He says that if she does not agree to the marriage, she will never again look him in the face. Juliet pleads with her mother for help. Her mother spurns her, and both parents storm out of the chamber.

Juliet turns to the Nurse for counsel, but is told only to marry Paris because Romeo's death is certain. Angered by the response, Juliet pretends to agree and says she is

The morning after the wedding night

going to see the Friar to make her confession. Juliet leaves, knowing that she can never again rely on the Nurse. She also realizes that if there is no other way out of this situation, she has the power to take her own life.

Analysis

This scene reiterates that, despite the strength of their love, Romeo and Juliet cannot fight time. Before they part, Juliet tries to pretend that daylight is not coming and that it is still nighttime. She is also the more realistic of the two. When the morning light is obvious, Juliet tells Romeo to leave. The vision that both of them have when they part, where they see one another pale as if they were dead, foreshadows what is to come, for this is the last moment they will spend alive together.

In this scene, Juliet grows to maturity. She dominates the conversation with her mother, who has no idea what she is talking about. She rejects her father's command to marry. She also realizes that the Nurse can no longer help. However, Juliet also becomes aware of her own lack of power. Why does she not just leave her father's household and go to Romeo in Mantua? She cannot do this because she is aware of her place in society and her father's right to control her.

Lady Capulet is brutally calculating, interested only in what will further the esteem of the household rather than in her daughter's feelings. Capulet himself is no longer the concerned father shown earlier. Now he emerges as an impulsive and even cruel man. His daughter is a commodity to be sold for her value.

Even the loyal Nurse has turned against Juliet. Her solution is easy: marry Paris because Romeo is doomed anyway. However, the Nurse's attitude is understandable to the audience. No matter how close the two are, the older woman is a servant to the Capulets; she is not family.

When Juliet recognizes that the Nurse can no longer be trusted and decides to see the Friar, she leaves her childhood behind. If the Friar will not help her, Juliet will be totally alone. She knows that her choices are limited. She also knows that if she cannot be with Romeo, she will take her life rather than marry Paris.

Act IV, Scene 1

Overview

Paris speaks to the Friar in his cell, revealing that Juliet's father has decided they should marry on Thursday to end Juliet's sadness over Tybalt's death. The Friar silently wishes he did not know the true reason the marriage should be delayed. Juliet enters. Although Paris speaks to her lovingly, he is also somewhat arrogant, as though she is already his wife. Juliet's response is neutral, and she seems indifferent to him, although she does remark that they are not yet married.

Paris leaves, thinking Juliet has come to the Friar for confession. But with knife in hand, Juliet tells the Friar that she will kill herself rather than marry Paris. However, the Friar has a plan. First, Juliet must outwardly agree to marry Paris. On the night before the wedding, the Friar will give Juliet a sleeping potion. After she drinks it, she will appear to be dead. The Friar will then send a message to Romeo.

Juliet and the Friar plan Juliet's fake death.

After Juliet is laid in the Capulet tomb, both Romeo and the Friar will be there when she awakens. Then the couple will go to Mantua to live together. Juliet agrees to this plan, and the Friar gives her a vial of the potion.

Analysis

The Friar is a wily character, although Shakespeare never presents him as such. Nor is he blamed for the tragedy that results from his plan. Interestingly, the plan demonstrates the play's constantly intertwined themes of life and death, love and marriage. The Friar uses his knowledge of herbs to make the potion that will put Juliet in a deathlike state. He is willing to help Juliet because of his own involvement in the situation. He has performed an illicit marriage and must now prevent a bigamous one.

Paris's feelings for Juliet are never fully explained, but he does assume, as do the Capulets, that Juliet's sadness is due to Tybalt's death. He also assumes that she wants to marry him. He knows nothing of her relationship with Romeo. Paris is never unkind to Juliet, although he does act as though she is his property. He is presented, however, as having some real feelings for her. Even so, his feelings for her terrify Juliet because she is already married and she does not love him.

Juliet has now matured fully. She has defied her father and is prepared to die if the Friar's plan does not work. She recognizes the danger, but is willing to take the risk in order to share her life with Romeo. This demonstrates not only her bravery, but the depth of her love.

Again the concepts of love and death are united in this scene. Juliet must appear to die in order to live and share her love with Romeo. Shakespeare has reversed the natural human cycle of birth to death. Here, death comes first—in the form of Juliet's trancelike state. If the Friar's plan hadn't turned out so wrong, from that apparent death a new life for the lovers would have emerged.

Act IV, Scene 2

Overview

Juliet returns home from seeing the Friar to find her parents together, preparing for the wedding. To their great surprise, she suddenly regrets her earlier outburst and quite cheerfully agrees to the marriage with Paris. In fact she is so cheerful that Capulet decides to move the ceremony up to Wednesday, the next day. Juliet agrees and tells the Nurse to find something for her to wear at the wedding. While she goes to her chamber (to drink the potion), Capulet runs off to tell Paris about the change in plans.

Analysis

Here again, time steps in to determine the lovers' fate. Juliet's feigned cheerfulness and her apparent willingness to accept the marriage to Paris cause her father to change the wedding plans again. It is now scheduled for the next day. This gives Juliet time to take the potion, but it also means that the Friar now has less time to notify Romeo about the plan. As the audience will learn, that delay will prove fatal.

Capulet has now become totally authoritative and arrogant. He believes that his wishes are being obeyed, so he demands an earlier marriage date. This requires that the staff work through the night to prepare for the wedding. He orders his wife around, telling her to go help the Nurse with the wedding preparations. He refers to his daughter as "peevish self-willed harlotry." He says he will stay up all night and take charge of the plans.

The difference between Juliet and her mother is especially striking here. Lady Capulet is shown as without power or respect and completely under the domination of her husband. But Juliet has taken control of her own life. While the household is in a frenzy over wedding preparations, she calmly retires to her chamber to take the potion. She has removed herself from her surroundings. She has placed her trust in the Friar and his plan, and her devotion to Romeo is absolute.

Act IV, Scene 3

Overview

In her chamber, Juliet tells the Nurse and her mother that she wishes to spend the night by herself. Thinking she needs some alone time, they depart. Her mother says, "Get thee to bed, and rest; for thou hast need." Now left alone and clutching the vial of sleeping potion, Juliet is overtaken by paranoia of the Friar's potion. She imagines herself buried alive in a tomb.

For a moment, the frightened thoughts continue. What if the Friar cannot be trusted? What if Romeo does not arrive on time? Suddenly she sees the ghost of Tybalt searching for Romeo. She weakens. However, the moment passes. She tells Tybalt's ghost to stop its search. She will be with Romeo. A resolute Juliet drinks the potion.

Tamara Rojo as Juliet in the ballet adaptation at the Royal Albert Hall, London

Analysis

The newfound strength of young Juliet reaches its climax. She understands the dangers facing her and the horrible consequences that could follow. But after an understandable moment of questioning, she accepts responsibility for her actions. She must trust the Friar. However, she also decides that if his plan fails and she does not go into a deathlike trance, she will be in charge of her life. To that end she places a dagger by her side before she drinks the potion. Previously, Juliet has mainly just reacted to those around her. She waited for Romeo to name the time of their marriage. She consented to her father's wishes. She trusted the Friar to come up with a plan. Now, no longer a child, she is a woman and a wife who will decide her own fate.

Act IV, Scene 4

Overview

It is early morning, and the Capulet household is astir with preparations. Lord Capulet has not yet been to bed, and he bustles around giving orders and shouting, "Make haste, make haste." The servants are excited. As daybreak approaches, he hears music. It signals that a group of musicians and Paris are on the way. Capulet tells the Nurse to get Juliet. As the scene ends, Capulet says, "The bridegroom he is come already."

Analysis

Capulet's last words are ironic, because Juliet already has a bridegroom, and it is not Paris. The frenzied atmosphere in the household contrasts sharply with the still body of Juliet, who lies in her bedchamber, apparently dead.

Act IV, Scene 5

Overview

The Nurse attempts to wake Juliet and finds her apparently dead. She screams for Capulet and Lady Capulet. The two come immediately, and all three despair over Juliet's

The Capulets discover the supposedly dead Juliet.

lifeless body. Shortly after, the Friar and Paris arrive, as do the musicians for the wedding. The Friar asks if the bride is ready for the church service (knowing full well she is not), and Capulet informs them that Juliet is dead.

The Friar joins in the sorrow, but tries to calm everyone by saying that Juliet is now in a better place. After much moaning, the Friar takes charge and asks everyone to "follow this fair corse [corpse] unto her grave." Everyone leaves except the Nurse and the musicians. Peter enters and asks the musicians to play a joyful tune to make him feel better. The musicians are aghast as such a request is inappropriate under the circumstances. There is some verbal sparring, and Peter leaves. The musicians, however, decide to wait until everyone returns so that they might get the lunch they were promised.

Analysis

Once again the Nurse's view of love and marriage turns to the sexual. As she goes to awaken Juliet, she says that the next night, "You shall rest but little." The audience, meanwhile, knows otherwise.

Paris's feelings for Juliet are shown here by his grief at her supposed death. His words seem to indicate a sense of personal loss rather than mere disappointment. The reactions of the Capulets also demonstrate genuine feelings for their daughter. Capulet speaks his most eloquent lines in the play when he says, "Death lies on her like an untimely frost / Upon the sweetest flower of all the field." It might also be argued that some of the Capulets' distress stems from the fact that they have lost the well-positioned Paris as a son-in-law.

Act V, Scene 1

Overview

Although banished, Romeo is joyful when he awakens on Wednesday morning in Mantua. He has just dreamed that Juliet discovered his dead body and her kiss brought him back to life. Then Balthasar, Romeo's trusted servant, enters and Romeo is happy to see him because he thinks the servant brings news that the Friar has told people in Verona about their marriage. "How fares my Juliet?" he says. "That I ask again, / For nothing can be ill if she be well." Balthasar responds with the terrible news that Juliet is dead. In a rage against fate, Romeo shouts, "I defy you, stars!"

Romeo says that he will return to Verona that evening. Then he suddenly thinks to ask Balthasar if there is a message from Friar Lawrence, but the servant says there is not. Balthasar leaves to hire horses for the journey.

Romeo buys poison from an apothecary.

Romeo now decides that he will kill himself in order to be with his beloved. He will lie with Juliet that very evening. He goes to an apothecary to get a vial of poison. The apothecary, however, refuses to sell it to him, saying that Mantua executes people who sell poison. Romeo can see that the man is obviously poor, so he offers the apothecary a large sum of money. The man then sells him the vial, which he guarantees will cause death: "Put this in any liquid thing you will / And drink it off, and if you had the strength / Of twenty men, it would dispatch you straight." With the poison in hand, Romeo is ready to return to Verona to kill himself at Juliet's tomb.

Analysis

Fate now takes charge of the lovers. Nothing can stop it. There is an outbreak of plague in the city. The Friar's messenger is forced into quarantine and cannot deliver the message about Juliet still being alive before Romeo leaves for Verona. Ironically, Balthasar was able to deliver the false message of Juliet's death. Balthasar arrives on the scene wearing boots, which, to Elizabethan audiences, was a signal of bad tidings.

The character of Romeo changes in this scene. Earlier, he raged against fate. Now his reaction to the terrible news of Juliet's death is the decision to take command of his life. He will join his beloved in death. The haste with which he makes this decision to die is one of many quick reactions—such as Romeo's fighting a duel after Mercutio's death, or Capulet's moving up the wedding day—that seal the fate of the characters.

Shakespeare uses the character of the apothecary to show how human traits play a part in the outcome of events. The apothecary says he can't sell the poison because it is illegal. But when he is offered a large sum of money, he does sell the poison because the society that makes the law also makes him poor.

Act V, Scene 2

Overview

In his cell, Friar Lawrence speaks with Friar John, who was sent to deliver the message to Romeo about the plan. Friar John explains that he was unable to leave a quarantined house and could not deliver the message. Not knowing that Romeo thinks Juliet is dead, Friar Lawrence fears that he will not be at Juliet's tomb according to the original plan. In three hours, Juliet will awaken. Someone must be there to rescue her. The Friar tells Friar John to get a crowbar and decides that he must rescue Juliet by himself, planning to keep her in his cell until Romeo arrives. He will send another message to Romeo in Mantua, explaining what has happened.

Analysis

Again, fate intervenes. There is desperation as Friar Lawrence realizes that Romeo has not received his letter. Now the Friar himself must take action. At this point only he can keep his plan from total destruction. But this sense of fate now also spellbinds the audience, which realizes—as the characters do not—that both Romeo and Juliet will die.

Act 5, Scene 3

Overview

It is night in the churchyard, and Paris enters with a servant, whom he sends off to keep watch. Then Paris spreads flowers on Juliet's grave. When he hears his page's signal, he moves off and hides. Romeo and Balthasar enter. Romeo carries a crowbar. He tells Balthasar that he is going to open the tomb in order to retrieve a ring that he had given to Juliet.

Upon discovering Romeo's dead body, Juliet commits suicide.

Romeo also tells Balthasar to leave and to deliver a letter he has written to his father in the morning. Balthasar retreats as ordered. However, he stays nearby because he has some doubts about what Romeo is up to.

Now Romeo opens Juliet's tomb. Paris, who is watching from his hiding place, recognizes Romeo as Tybalt's killer. Since Paris believes that Juliet died from grief over Tybalt's death, he marks Romeo as Juliet's killer also. But why has Romeo returned from banishment to visit the Capulet tomb? Paris reasons that Romeo's hatred toward the Capulets is so great that he is willing to dishonor their gravesite. Enraged, Paris leaps out from his hiding place.

Romeo tries to stop the attack, but Paris will not be turned away. The two men draw their swords as Paris's servant runs off to find the watchman. In the fight, Romeo mortally wounds Paris. As Paris dies, he asks Romeo to be merciful and put his body in the tomb with Juliet.

Romeo agrees and places Paris in the tomb. As he does so, he looks at Juliet's body and wonders how she can look so beautiful in death. He tells her that he has come to spend eternity with her. Romeo drinks the poison and says, "Thus with a kiss I die."

Friar Lawrence enters the graveyard carrying a crowbar, spade, and lantern. He meets Balthasar, who tells him that Romeo must be in the tomb. Balthasar says he fell asleep in his hiding place but had a dream that Romeo had a fight with someone. The Friar enters the tomb and finds the bodies of Paris and Romeo. As he is lamenting this tragedy, Juliet rises and asks for Romeo.

The Friar tells her that both Paris and Romeo are dead and that the watch is coming. She must leave immediately. But when Juliet says she will not go, the Friar leaves without her. Alone, Juliet sees the vial of poison that Romeo drank. Thinking the poison might also kill her, she kisses Romeo. Now the watchmen and Paris's servant enter. As they approach, she quickly takes Romeo's dagger and stabs herself. Juliet falls and dies.

There is much excitement as the watchmen view the bodies and also find the Friar and Balthasar nearby. Prince Escalus enters, followed by the Capulets and then Montague. He says that Lady Montague has died from grief over her son's banishment. The Capulets and Montague view their dead children. The prince asks what has happened, and Friar Lawrence recounts the story of the secret marriage and the plan that failed. Balthasar gives the letter written by Romeo to the prince, backing up the Friar's story.

The prince turns to Capulet and Montague, blaming them for the tragedy. Thus rebuked, Capulet and Montague shake hands. They vow to build gold statues of their lost children and to end the feud. The words of the prince end the tragedy: "For never was a story of more woe / Than this of Juliet and her Romeo."

Analysis

It is ironic that the feud ends. By their deaths, Romeo and Juliet created the very world in which they would have been allowed to live and love. The audience senses this tragedy. The two young people become the symbols of true love because they were willing to sacrifice everything. The lives of Romeo and Juliet are immortalized, but immortality seems empty because their triumph comes only in death. Their tragedy is that, in order to preserve their love, they must choose death.

It is interesting that the possibility of suicide is mentioned throughout the play. The love between Romeo and Juliet is intense. If it cannot be fulfilled, then they believe the only alternative is death, for neither can live without the other. At various times, both Romeo and Juliet express the feeling that if they cannot have their love, they are willing to die for it.

Appropriately, the last scene takes place in the darkness. The two lovers have spent nearly all their time together in the dark. Now they will spend eternity there together.

Analysis of Major Characters

Romeo

Romeo is a much-debated character in English literature. Some critics argue that he is an erratic teenager, more in love with love than with any actual person. His passion-filled longings for the indifferent Rosaline seem juvenile. If he is not riding a cloud of euphoria, he is in the depths of total despair. Yet, immediately upon meeting Juliet, all thoughts of Rosaline vanish. From that moment on, Romeo's feelings for Juliet grow into an intense and profound passion—how realistic readers find this is open to interpretation.

Moderation is not a word in Romeo's vocabulary. Intelligent and quick-witted, he acts upon his emotions, a trait that contributes to the tragic fate of the young lovers. He sneaks into the forbidden Capulet garden to catch a glimpse of Juliet. He refuses to fight Tybalt because they are now related through marriage, but this results in his friend Mercutio's death. That compels Romeo to kill Tybalt to avenge Mercutio's death. When he is banished from Verona, Romeo wails on the floor of the Friar's cell and halfheartedly tries to commit suicide. But when the Friar devises a plan, Romeo becomes calm and rational. And when he is told of Juliet's supposed death, he does not wail but calmly resolves to end his life to be with her.

In this great tragedy, both Romeo and Juliet can be seen as either representative of extreme youth and inexperience, or victims of fate, two people who have reached a level of passionate love that overshadows all else. Although *Romeo and Juliet* may be a tragedy, it is above all a love story.

Juliet

The emphasis throughout the play is on Juliet's youth. She is not yet fourteen, but is forced by fate to make adult decisions. At the opening, Juliet is an obedient girl who respects the wishes of her parents. When her mother says that Paris wishes to marry her, Juliet responds by saying that she will see if she can love him. Furthermore, at thirteen she is understandably uncomfortable with explicit early discussions of sex, as seen in her embarrassment when the Nurse tells a sexual joke. However, the strength of her character emerges in that scene with her mother and the Nurse.

After meeting Romeo at the feast, Juliet begins to develop her own feelings and opinions about her destiny. She willingly defies her parents and goes so far as to marry Romeo in secret. When Romeo is banished for killing Tybalt, Juliet is forced to choose between love and family. She makes the tough decision that her loyalty will be to Romeo. In doing so, she cuts all of the ties that bind her to her family and the Nurse. Her growing strength is further shown in Act IV, when she agrees to swallow a potion rather than enter into a bigamous marriage with Paris. Her decision to take her own life, when she awakens to find that Romeo has died, stems from the strength of her love for him. Her own suicide is a test of her resolve, in that she is able to stab herself with a dagger. The complexity of her character is based on whether we see her as a teenager who is ruled by her impulses, or as a young girl looking to determine her own future.

Friar Lawrence

Friar Lawrence is seemingly a minor character in the play. He is a kindhearted cleric, adviser to both Romeo and Juliet, and the play's only religious figure. Yet it is the Friar who is responsible for the tragic developments that take place. It is his schemes that move the action along. Although he means well, his actions lead to the tragedy that ensues.

At first the Friar is not convinced of Romeo's feelings for Juliet, judging that Romeo has been too hasty in declaring his devotion. However, he soon agrees to the marriage, mainly because he hopes the union will end the feud. Thus the Friar's role becomes one of peacemaker. He does not yet believe that Romeo and Juliet are in love, but he sanctions the marriage, hoping it will bring peace.

The Friar's somewhat mystical knowledge of plants is never explained, and it seems unusual for a Catholic cleric. But this knowledge plays an important role in the play. When the Friar comes up with the plan to give Juliet a potion, he is attempting to help the lovers. But he is also trying to correct his mistakes. He has married the two; he cannot, as a religious man, sanction Juliet's double

A Feud Between Two Households

VIOLENCE AND HATE flow freely throughout the play. They are key themes and provide the main motivation for many characters. The cause of the feud between the Capulets and Montagues is never explained or even discussed. It clearly is no longer important to the characters, and instead the mere fact of previous hatred is used as an excuse for continuing hatred and violence.

Fighting on Verona's streets

Gangs and blood in *West Side Story*

Violence and tribalism are often emphasized in modern adaptations of the play. Tribalism means a loyalty to one's own group and an instinctive dislike of other groups. Two famous film examples are the 1961 musical *West Side Story* and 1996's modernized take called *Romeo + Juliet*. *West Side Story* reimagines the Montagues and Capulets as street gangs from opposing racial groups. *Romeo + Juliet* also uses gangs, but sets the action in millennial California where spoiled rich kids act out in brawls the rivalry between their parents' companies.

Guns and knives feature prominently in both films. The kids of *Romeo + Juliet* carry handguns like cell phones, with brand names such as "Rapier" and "Sword 9mm." This is both a clever way to fit references to swords into a modern setting, and also emphasize the cavalier way these youthful gangs treat violence and death. In *West Side Story*, the violence is more realistic in many ways due to its intimacy. Fights are carried out with bats and switchblades, and it is only at the film's climax that guns make an appearance. Everything is done at close quarters, with characters often dying in each other's arms.

The genius of these interpretations is their ability to convey how, in the play, death is a real possibility for all characters at all times. Hatred closes down reason and robs people of their control. It is a reminder that it was not fate alone that killed Romeo and Juliet.

marriage to Paris. So he devises the plan to bring about her apparent death and subsequent revival.

In the scene where Juliet is discovered and presumed dead, the Friar shows himself capable of dishonesty. He hurries the families to accept the false death and complete the burial. Yet, at the end of the play, the Friar reacts weakly; he runs from the tomb, leaving behind the drugged Juliet.

Friar Lawrence is a well-meaning and kind man. He is also a person capable of making the wrong choices for the right reasons. Like all the other characters in the play, he succumbs to the ultimate tragedy. However, more than most, it is the Friar who helps bring about the tragedy.

Nurse

The role of the Nurse is important. As the beginning, she is a confidante for Juliet, and as the action progresses, she becomes the go-between for the lovers. She is also the only character besides the Friar who knows about the marriage. The Nurse is a comic foil to Juliet; that is, she is someone who brings out the main qualities of another character.

The contrast between the Nurse and Juliet is striking. The older woman is coarse, speaking with many bawdy references to the physical side of love. She loves Juliet as a daughter but has no understanding of the intense feelings between her charge and Romeo. The relationship between the two women keeps the focus on Juliet's age. The Nurse is old and constantly complains about her physical ailments. But her sexual remarks and ongoing patter introduce a feeling of lightheartedness within the tragedy of the play.

Initially, the Nurse is Juliet's close confidante. She becomes a conspirator when Juliet confides her love for

Romeo and her plan to marry him. The Nurse wants only happiness for the young girl. But when Romeo kills Tybalt and is banished, the Nurse sees trouble ahead. Therefore she advises Juliet to forget about Romeo and marry Paris, even though she is aware that Juliet is already married. By suggesting a false marriage, the Nurse loses Juliet's trust. Juliet now turns to the Friar for advice, and the Nurse is no longer included in her plans.

Like the Friar, the Nurse is a central character in moving the action along. She is the one who identifies Romeo and Juliet for each other at the feast. She carries messages between the two. She brings the news to Juliet that Romeo has killed Tybalt and has been banished. She arranges for the wedding night. Finally, she tells Juliet to marry Paris and loses her role as confidante.

Chapter Three

A Closer Look

Themes

The Power of Love

The power of love and its consequences are evident throughout. It is the most famous love story in English literature. But such love is not for the faint of heart. The love that develops between Romeo and Juliet is all-powerful, even brutal. It is an overwhelming emotion that leads these young people to their own destruction. Love makes them defy the normal boundaries of their world.

Juliet defies her father by secretly marrying Romeo and angers her father when she appears reluctant to marry Paris. Romeo defies authority by breaking his exile and returning to Verona when Balthasar brings him news of Juliet's supposed death.

Shakespeare explores the different kinds of love in this play. There is love based on sexual pleasure. The Nurse speaks of this type of love, as does Mercutio. There is the

Romeo and Juliet painted by Ford Madox Brown

so-called love that is actually infatuation, demonstrated by Romeo's desire for Rosaline. It is often argued Romeo is in love solely with the idea and the passion of love. There is the love brought from circumstances. Paris is "a good catch" for the Capulet family, and he does exhibit a kind of ownership over Juliet during the drama. However, he does give the sense that he has feelings for her, especially at the end, when he is mortally wounded. Finally, there is the instantaneous and overwhelming love between Romeo and Juliet, sometimes believed to be true love. Beyond just a feeling, this love produces a willingness to do anything to obtain and keep it. This all-encompassing passion, coupled with the other main themes of the play, leads to its tragic conclusion.

Hate Versus Love

Love cannot exist without hate in *Romeo and Juliet*. Both love and hate determine the fate of the characters. The love between Romeo and Juliet is matched in power by the hatred between their two families. The cause of the bitter feud is never explained. Presumably, had their family differences been solved earlier, the tragedy of Romeo and Juliet would never have taken place.

Capulet and Montague kinsmen start fights in the streets.

Hate begins the trouble for the two lovers when Tybalt sees Romeo at the feast and believes Romeo is present to mock the celebration. Tybalt later sees Romeo on the street and insults him. When Romeo refuses to fight and Mercutio fights and dies, Romeo feels that he must fight Tybalt, which results in his banishment.

Even Juliet is affected by the atmosphere of hate that surrounds everyone. When her cousin Tybalt is killed by Romeo, she experiences a moment of doubt about her lover, but when the Nurse speaks against Romeo, Juliet is quick to defend him. Hate affects not only the main characters of the play, but also all of the supporting cast. The hatred between Montague and Capulet household servants leads to street brawls. It is as forceful as love in moving the action of the play.

The Certainty of Fate

Fate underlines all of the action of the play. In the prologue, the Chorus speaks of "star-cross'd lovers." Their destinies are controlled by the stars, something that the characters themselves understand and accept. At the false news of Juliet's death, Romeo cries, "Then I defy you, stars" (Act V, Scene 1). He is acknowledging that their love is opposed by destiny, or fate.

It is perhaps easy to blame everything that happens on bad luck. What if Tybalt hadn't recognized Romeo at the feast? What if Romeo hadn't met Tybalt on the street and refused to fight? What if Mercutio hadn't been so hot-tempered? What if there wasn't an epidemic of plague at the time and the letter to Romeo in Mantua had been delivered? What if Romeo had waited a few more minutes before he drank the poison? But there are no "what ifs" to this story; fate has taken control.

Especially in Elizabethan times, the idea of fate played an important role in people's lives. Many believed it was unchangeable. Unfortunately for Romeo and Juliet, they fall in love with "the enemy." The Friar's plan to give Juliet a potion and then unite the lovers goes wrong because of the plague that prevents the message from being delivered to Romeo. Fate interferes with the timing at Juliet's grave, when Romeo takes poison and dies only moments before Juliet awakens.

However fate can also be seen as a force that, while influencing human decisions, does not control them completely. Human personalities and weaknesses also play a role.

In Act III, Scene 1, Romeo bemoans the death of his friend Mercutio and blames fate. But when Tybalt enters and feels no remorse at Mercutio's death, Romeo makes a choice. He decides that one of them must die to avenge Mercutio: "Either thou or I, or both, must go with him." When the two fight and Tybalt dies, Romeo, who cannot accept what he has done, reverts to fate once again: "O, I am fortune's fool!"

The final terrible fated moment occurs when Juliet wakes and compounds Romeo's death by taking her own life. But just as she is gaining consciousness, the Friar leaves her alone because he hears the watch coming. Had he stayed with her, Juliet's death might have been prevented. The consequences of fate may be unalterable in *Romeo and Juliet*, but they are also influenced by human decisions and weaknesses.

Motifs

Two important motifs in *Romeo and Juliet* are the imagery of light and dark, and the use of time. Shakespeare uses light or its absence to contribute to the mood of the scenes. Because of their circumstances, the lovers must spend most of their time together in darkness. But in their case and throughout the play, dark is not always evil and light does not always convey good.

Light and dark images recur often in conversations between Romeo and Juliet. When Romeo first sees Juliet at the feast, (Act I, Scene 5) he is moved to remark:

> *O, she doth teach the torches to burn bright!*
> *It seems she hangs upon the cheek of night …*

But the most quoted use of light and dark imagery occurs in the famous Balcony Scene (Act II, Scene 2). After comparing Juliet to the sun, Romeo blurs day and night:

> *The brightness of her cheek would*
> *shame those stars*
> *As daylight doth a lamp …*

Day and night is a vivid motif after the lovers spend their only night together (Act III, Scene 5). Now the light must be feared because it means they must part, sending Romeo into exile. They both try to keep the light from filling Juliet's chamber.

But when they cannot deny that morning is upon them, Juliet says, "O, now be gone! More light and light it grows." Romeo answers, "More light and light; more dark and dark our woes." At the end of the play, the tragic consequences are entirely buried in darkness. Prince Escalus speaks these words over their bodies:

> *A glooming peace this morning with it brings.*
> *The sun, for sorrow, will not show his head.*

The motif of time is evident in both the plot and the language of Romeo and Juliet. Shakespeare compresses the play's time span into four days. There are numerous references to time throughout, starting in the Prologue of Act I when the Chorus remarks: "The fearful passage of their death-marked love … Is now the two hours' traffic of our stage." In addition, numerous characters frequently refer to time, citing specific hours or days of the week. In this way, the audience is kept aware of how quickly time passes and how important it is to the story's development.

After their first meeting, the love between the two young people develops at an accelerated pace. Juliet recognizes this in Act II, Scene 2, noting: "It is too rash, too unadvised, too sudden, / Too like the lightning, which doth cease to be / Ere one can say it lightens." After Romeo's banishment, time becomes an enemy. Capulet speeds up Juliet's marriage date to Paris. Because of the hasty marriage plans, Friar Lawrence makes up the potion as a way to unite the lovers. But in the end, time catches up with Romeo and Juliet and eventually overtakes their lives. In their death, however, they defeat time and remain forever united in love.

Time is also connected to the motif of light and dark. There are many references throughout the play to the moon, sun, and stars. These references help create the sense of day and night. That is important because so much of the interplay between Romeo and Juliet must necessarily take place in darkness.

Symbols

In *Romeo and Juliet*, poison is a symbol of death. The Friar makes a potion for Juliet that appears to bring on death. It does not do that, but it does, without intention, bring about Romeo's suicide.

In Shakespeare's play, poison is not evil of itself. As the Friar says in Act II, Scene 3, plants and herbs have special purposes in nature. They can be used for good or bad. It is human intent that can turn a potion sold by the apothecary for healing into a poison that instead causes death. Shakespeare shows poison to be a weapon for desperate people.

Foreshadowing is another strong element throughout the play. At various times the characters are overcome by bad feelings. These feelings are symbols of their tragic fate. The use of foreshadowing provides subtle clues and assures the audience of what will indeed happen. It also pulls the audience along as the plot thickens. For instance, Romeo has some bad feelings on his way to the Capulet feast (Act I, Scene 4):

> *I fear, too early; for my mind misgives*
> *Some consequence yet hanging in the stars …*

These bad feelings confirm what the audience knows; Romeo will meet Juliet and begin the chain of events that leads to their deaths. Each time a character shows worry, it is one more assurance of the inevitable ending.

Foreshadowing occurs time and again throughout the play. In Act I, Scene 5, Tybalt has to obey his uncle and not attack Romeo at the feast. But the hot-tempered Tybalt does not forget what he sees as an insult:

Daggers and poison are the weapons of the day.

I will withdraw. But this intrusion shall,
Now seeming sweet, convert to bitt'rest gall.

This tells the audience that Tybalt is going to cause trouble, which he eventually does, causing Mercutio's death and bringing on his own.

In that same scene, Juliet wants the Nurse to find out Romeo's name because she is afraid he is married:

Go ask his name. If he be married,
My grave is like to be my wedding bed.

Juliet is saying that she will never marry if she cannot have Romeo. But the audience knows her grave will indeed become her wedding bed.

In Act II, Scene 3, the Friar worries that Romeo is rushing too quickly into marriage: "Wisely and slow; they stumble that run fast." In Act IV, Scene 3, Juliet worries about the potion that the Friar has made for her: "What if it be a poison, which the friar / Subtly hath minister'd to have me dead." In these scenes, Shakespeare repeatedly tells the audience that fate has the upper hand.

Language

In all his plays, Shakespeare used three forms of language: prose, rhymed verse, and blank verse.

Prose is ordinary speech, but it is not necessarily spoken only by the lower classes. There is no particular rhythm pattern and the lines don't have the same number of syllables. Shakespeare used prose for simple explanations of a situation, scenes of everyday life, or just relaxed conversation. One example is in Act I, Scene 1. Two

Capulet servants, Sampson and Gregory, see two servants from the hated Montague household approaching. They speak in prose to decide how to insult the incomers.

Shakespeare uses prose in many of the scenes throughout the play. The characters in Act II, Scene 4, and Act III, Scene 1, for instance, speak mainly in prose. An example is the Nurse's agitated conversation with Romeo when she is trying to arrange a meeting. The Nurse's speech is also an example where the use of prose does indicate the lower class of the speaker, as well as its humorous effect.

Rhymed verse is usually in the form of two lines whose ending words rhyme with each other. For instance, referring to Rosaline, Romeo speaks this rhymed verse at the end of Act I, Scene 2:

> *I'll go along, no such sight to be shown,*
> *But to rejoice in splendor of mine own.*

Shakespeare often used rhymed verse in prologues and in passages that give advice or are very lyrical. Act II, Scene 3, contains only rhymed verse. In part of this passage, Friar Lawrence expresses his surprise at how quickly Romeo has turned his attention away from the fair Rosaline:

> *Holy Saint Francis! What a change is here!*
> *Is Rosaline, that thou didst love so dear,*
> *So soon forsaken? Young men's love then lies*
> *Not truly in their hearts, but in their eyes.*

The play also finishes (Act V, Scene 3) with two rhymed lines, called a rhyming couplet. They are spoken by Prince Escalus:

For never was a story of more woe
Than this of Juliet and her Romeo.

Blank verse refers to unrhymed iambic pentameter. That means most lines have ten syllables. They alternate between stressed and unstressed syllables. Like prose, the last words in the lines don't rhyme in any regular pattern. But you can tell blank verse from prose by reading it aloud. It has a regular pattern. Romeo's opening speech to Juliet in the famous balcony scene is in blank verse, which begins: "But soft! What light through yonder window breaks?" You can also tell blank verse by looking at it. The first word in each line is capitalized, and not all the lines are the same length or fill the page. In Shakespeare's plays, blank verse is used because it closely resembles the natural speaking patterns of English. It also marks great occasions. Many of Shakespeare's most famous speeches are written in blank verse.

Act III, Scene 4, contains only blank verse, as do Act IV, Scenes 3 and 4, and Act V, Scene 2. In the latter, Friar Lawrence finds out that Friar John was not able to deliver the message to Romeo about the potion Friar Lawrence gave to Juliet. Friar Lawrence is now faced with a problem:

Unhappy fortune! By my brotherhood,
The letter was not nice but full of charge,
Of dear import, and the neglecting it
May do much danger. Friar John, go hence;
Get me an iron crow and bring it straight
Unto my cell.

The language is one of the most compelling aspects of *Romeo and Juliet*. The characters jest and curse, scream at each other, and beat their chests in emotional anguish. Puns and witty sexual references abound. It is a splendid linguistic show.

It Is the East, and Juliet Is the Sun

This is probably the play's most famous and oft-quoted scene. Romeo stands below, looking up at Juliet on the balcony (or at the window). He speaks of his passion for her in what is often thought of as the epitome of romantic expression. Remember that this is blank verse and is meant to be read in a regular pattern. The speech is flowery, even for that time, and full of symbols. These lines are to be read with the understanding that Shakespeare uses such methods to convey the extent of Romeo's feelings. After hearing the speech, the audience is aware that this is nothing like his musings over the fair Rosaline; it is nothing like anything Romeo has ever experienced. The very depth that this speech conveys is the underlying reason that both of the lovers are willing to—and do—die for their love. Without that understanding, the audience cannot comprehend the tragedy that ensues.

Romeo pours out his heart, first by comparing Juliet to the sunrise. He likens the window of her chamber to the eastern horizon at dawn:

But soft! What light through
yonder window breaks?
It is the east, and Juliet is the sun.

Romeo implores Juliet to appear at the window, telling her that the moon (actually the moon goddess Diana) is sad because Juliet's beauty is greater than hers, just as the sun's light is greater than that of the moon:

Arise, fair sun, and kill the envious moon,
Who is already sick and pale with grief
That thou, her maid, art far more fair than she.

Romeo says that Juliet must no longer serve the virginal moon goddess, who is jealous of her:

Be not her maid, since she is envious;
Her vestal livery is but sick and green,
And none but fools do wear it; cast it off.

And now, Juliet actually appears at the window, and Romeo is struck with her beauty.

Romeo cannot hear Juliet, but he talks himself into thinking she is talking to him:

She speaks, yet she says nothing. What of that?
Her eye discourses; I will answer it.

Presumably he takes a step toward the window, then realizes she is unaware of his presence below:

I am too bold; 'tis not to me she speaks.

So, once more, he returns to the imagery of light. He says that the two most beautiful stars in the heavens should ask Juliet's eyes to take their place:

Two of the fairest stars in all the heaven,

Having some business, do entreat her eyes
To twinkle in their spheres till they return.
What if her eyes were there, they in her head?

He continues to compare her beauty to nature's light, saying that her eyes could change night into day and make the birds sing. Then, like many young men in love, he becomes even more poetic and dazzled by Juliet's beauty:

See how she leans her cheek upon her hand!
O, that I were a glove upon that hand,
That I might touch that cheek!

In the opening lines, Romeo calls Juliet the sun. Even the moon, often regarded as a symbol of feminine beauty, is envious of her. But none of these lines is meant to be taken literally. Romeo is well aware that Juliet is not the sun. He knows the moon is not jealous of her. But he uses these symbols of light and beauty to show that, for him, Juliet surpasses them all.

Note the use of comparisons throughout the speech. Besides comparing her to the sun and moon, he says Juliet's eyes are fairer than the stars in heaven. They are so fair that the brightness of her cheek outshines them, so fair that the birds think daylight has come.

Interpreting the Play

Historical Context

Shakespeare probably wrote *Romeo and Juliet* in the early 1590s. The exact date is unknown. In Act I, Scene 3, the Nurse talks of an earthquake: "'Tis since the earthquake now eleven years." There was an earthquake in England in

1580, which would put the writing at 1591. Most experts, however, think the play was written later.

Shakespeare acknowledges the plague in *Romeo and Juliet*. In fact it plays a large role in determining the fate of the lovers. Because of the plague quarantine, the message about Juliet and the potion never reaches Romeo.

Influences of *Romeo and Juliet*

Romeo and Juliet has been staged, performed, written about, sung about, imitated, modernized, and endlessly discussed. It is the world's ultimate love story. Its influence on all subsequent romantic literature is enormous. The words *Romeo* and *lover* mean the same thing in the English-speaking world. To call a young man "Romeo" indicates that he is highly attractive to the opposite sex. The actresses who played the female title role were known for wearing a "Juliet cap," a wedding headband that holds the veil. Both of the title characters have become symbols of romantic and passionate love, of young love, and of those who defy authority for a greater goal.

Along with *Hamlet*, *Romeo and Juliet* ranks as one of Shakespeare's most-performed plays. The London theaters were closed for a time by the Puritans in 1642 but reopened in 1660 when the monarchy was restored. Two years later, Henry Harris starred as Romeo, with Mary Saunderson playing Juliet. She was probably the first woman to play the role, as young boys had played the part until then. But there were all sorts of changes made to the play thereafter. Some versions changed the ending, so the young lovers did not die. Another had Juliet awaken just before Romeo died. Another changed the setting to ancient Rome, and some toned down Shakespeare's sexual language. It was not until 1845 that the original version returned to the stage in the United States and shortly afterward in England.

In 1935, the renowned English actors John Gielgud and Laurence Olivier played the roles of Romeo and Mercutio. After a six-week run, they exchanged parts. In 1986, the Royal Shakespeare Company set the play in present-day Verona. In this souped-up version, the feast becomes a rock party with drugs, the men fight with switchblades instead of swords, and Romeo dies not from a dagger but from a hypodermic needle.

Shakespeare's masterpiece also influenced the world of opera and ballet. Of the many operas based on the famous play, the best known is Charles Gounod's *Romeo et Juliette*, first performed in 1867. The 2004–2005 season of the Paris Opera Ballet included the classic love story, which featured the work of two other legends besides Shakespeare. This production used the choreography of the great ballet dancer Rudolf Nureyev. The Russian-born Nureyev, who died in 1993, had first choreographed *Romeo and Juliet* in 1977 for the London Festival Ballet. Critics said his version more closely followed Shakespeare's story than most others do. The choreography was complemented by the masterful score of Romantic composer Sergei Prokofiev's version, which had debuted in 1938.

In addition, *Romeo and Juliet* is certainly no stranger to the silver screen, having been filmed numerous times, beginning in the silent era. The 1936 version received four Oscar nominations but has not stood the test of time, possibly because the stars Norma Shearer and Leslie Howard were much older than the original lovers. Franco Zeffirelli's 1968 film is an exciting and colorful version, and a good introduction to visualize the play. Regrettably,

Age Is Just a Number, Right?

JULIET IS A difficult character to interpret for many reasons, one big reason being her age. Age and youth come into constant conflict throughout the drama, but audience perceptions of age and "age-appropriate" behavior can also have a massive effect on how we interpret the characters' actions.

Juliet is often described as a character who starts off young and naive, and later blossoms into maturity as fate forces her to make decisions. It is she who slows down Romeo's outbursts and gets him to state his intentions. She creates most of the initial plans. Romeo, in comparison, is rash and impetuous. He claims that love for Juliet has overtaken his soul, yet five minutes earlier he was desperately in love with Rosaline. Who's to say there wasn't yet another girl beforehand that he immediately forgot upon meeting Rosaline?

Shakespeare's source material for the play, an old European love story, placed Juliet as between sixteen and eighteen years old.

So why did Shakespeare change it? Some critics have argued that by changing her age, Shakespeare wanted Juliet to appear more vulnerable, providing greater contrast with the strength of her later actions. Others still have said he was merely reflecting the contemporary Italian culture, which believed girls to be sexually mature at a younger age.

Modern adaptations have struggled with Juliet's age. Most film versions show Juliet at fifteen or sixteen. This raises some interesting questions about the play. How can a thirteen-year-old be ready for marriage and children? Can a thirteen-year-old really fall in love? And finally, if we think not, is Juliet really maturing throughout the play or simply swept up in her emotions and impulses? If *Romeo and Juliet* is not true love, does this make their fate any less tragic?

however, Zeffirelli spends most of the time on the first half of the tragedy, understating the importance of the development of Juliet's maturity. In this version, Romeo and Juliet are seventeen and fifteen, respectively. Baz Luhrmann directed a hip adaptation of the play in the 1996 film *Romeo + Juliet* starring Leonardo DiCaprio and Claire Danes. Set in the California suburb of Verona, the film's script retains Shakespeare's original dialogue.

The most famous musical adaptation in the Broadway theater (1957) and on film (1961) is *West Side Story*, with music by Leonard Bernstein and lyrics by Stephen Sondheim. In this updated retelling, the Montagues and Capulets become the Jets and the Sharks, rival gangs in Manhattan, and the ill-fated lovers are ex-Jet Tony and Maria, the Puerto Rican sister of the Sharks' gang leader. The Broadway run lasted 732 performances; the Hollywood version took ten Oscars, and a special award went to Jerome Robbins for choreography. Shakespeare lives on.

Tone

The tone of a play doesn't refer to *what* is said or done; it refers to *how*. Tone comes from language, symbols, diction, images, syntax (the rules of grammar), and allusion (references to a person, place, or event). In other words, the tone of a play results from the play's many parts.

In *Romeo and Juliet*, there are obvious and dramatic changes of tone throughout the play. In Act II, Scene 2, for example, everything is romantic and hopeful as the lovers speak in the Capulet orchard. Romeo and Juliet express their love and desire to be together. The images of passionate and enduring love abound. But by the end of Act II, in Scene 6, there is an aura of encroaching doom. This is a short scene that ends with the lovers being married by the Friar. Even as he wishes to be married to Juliet, Romeo speaks of death, saying that not even death can take away the pleasure he feels in this marriage.

Almost immediately as the curtain opens on Act III, the tone of doom widens into an atmosphere of bursting tempers, sharp discourse, and sudden violence. When Tybalt asks to speak to a Capulet, Mercutio immediately responds with a threat: "And but one word with one of us? Couple it with something; make it a word and blow." The fiery Tybalt replies, "You shall find me apt enough to that, sir, an you will give me occasion." When Romeo refuses to draw his sword, the hot-tempered Mercutio immediately answers Tybalt's challenge: "Will you pluck your sword out of his pilcher by the ears? Make haste, lest mine be about your ears ere it be out." When Mercutio is wounded, his usual banter and wit sharply change: "Ask for me tomorrow, and you shall find me a grave man."

These and many other instances of tone differences throughout the play help move the action along. They are indicators of what lies ahead. With each clever shift in tone, the audience comes to realize that the circumstances surrounding the two lovers are about to change and nothing will stop the course of tragic events.

CHRONOLOGY

1564 William Shakespeare is born on April 23 in Stratford-upon-Avon, England

1578–1582 Span of Shakespeare's "Lost Years," covering the time between leaving school and marrying Anne Hathaway of Stratford

1582 At age eighteen, Shakespeare marries Anne Hathaway, age twenty-six, on November 28

1583 Susanna Shakespeare, William and Anne's first child, is born in May, six months after the wedding

1584 Birth of twins Hamnet and Judith Shakespeare

1585–1592 Shakespeare leaves his family in Stratford to become an actor and playwright in a London theater company

1587 Public beheading of Mary Queen of Scots

1593–1594 The Bubonic (Black) Plague closes theaters in London

1594–1596 As a leading playwright, Shakespeare creates some of his most popular works, including *A Midsummer Night's Dream* and *Romeo and Juliet*

1596 Hamnet Shakespeare dies in August at age eleven, possibly of plague

1596–1597 *The Merchant of Venice* and *Henry IV, Part One* are most likely written

1599 The Globe Theatre opens

1600 *Julius Caesar* is first performed at the Globe

1600–1601 *Hamlet* is believed to have been written

1601–1602 *Twelfth Night* is probably composed

1603 Queen Elizabeth dies; Scottish king James VI succeeds her and becomes England's James I

1604 Shakespeare pens *Othello*

1605 *Macbeth* is composed

1608–1610 London's theaters are forced to close when the plague returns and kills an estimated thirty-three thousand people

1611 *The Tempest* is written

1613 The Globe Theatre is destroyed by fire

1614 The reopening of the Globe

1616 Shakespeare dies on April 23

1623 Anne Hathaway, Shakespeare's widow, dies; a collection of Shakespeare's plays, known as the First Folio, is published

A SHAKESPEARE GLOSSARY

addition A name or title, such as knight, duke, duchess, king, etc.

affect To like or love; to be attracted to.

approve To prove or confirm.

attend To pay attention.

belike Probably.

beseech To beg or request.

bondman A slave.

bootless Futile; useless; in vain.

broil A battle.

charge Expense, responsibility; to command or accuse.

common A term describing the common people, below nobility.

condition Social rank; quality.

countenance Face; appearance; favor.

cousin A relative.

curious Careful; attentive to detail.

discourse To converse; conversation.

discover To reveal or uncover.

dispatch To speed or hurry; to send; to kill.

doubt To suspect.

entreat To beg or appeal.

envy To hate or resent; hatred; resentment.

ere Before.

eyne Eyes.

fain Gladly.

fare To eat; to prosper.

favor Face, privilege.

fellow A peer or equal.

filial Of a child toward its parent.

fine An end; "in fine" means in sum.

folio A book made up of individually printed sheets, each folded in half to make four pages. Shakespeare's folios contain all of his known plays in addition to other works.

fond Foolish.

fool A darling.

genius A good or evil spirit.

gentle Well-bred; not common.

gentleman One whose labor was done by servants. (Note: to call someone a *gentleman* was not a mere compliment on his manners; it meant that he was above the common people.)

gentles People of quality.

get To beget (a child).

go to "Go on"; "come off it."

go we Let us go.

haply Perhaps.

happily By chance; fortunately.

hard by Nearby.

heavy Sad or serious.

husbandry Thrift; economy.

instant Immediate.

kind One's nature; species.

knave A villain; a poor man.

lady A woman of high social rank. (Note: *lady* was not a synonym for *woman* or *polite woman*; it was not a compliment but simply a word referring to one's actual legal status in society, like *gentleman*.)

leave Permission; "take my leave" means depart (with permission).

lief, lieve "I had as lief" means I would just as soon; I would rather.

like To please; "it likes me not" means it is disagreeable to me.

livery The uniform of a nobleman's servants; emblem.

Lord Chamberlain's Men The company of players Shakespeare joined in London; under James I they became the King's Men.

mark Notice; pay attention.

morrow Morning.

needs Necessarily.

nice Too fussy or fastidious.

owe To own.

passing Very.

peculiar Individual; exclusive.

privy Private; secret.

proper Handsome; one's very own ("his proper son").

protest To insist or declare.

quite Completely.

require Request.

several Different, various.

severally Separately.

sirrah A term used to address social inferiors.

sooth Truth.

state Condition; social rank.

still Always; persistently.

success Result(s).

surfeit Fullness.

touching Concerning; about; as for.

translate To transform.

unfold To disclose.

verse Writing that uses a regular metrical rhythm and is divided from other lines by a space.

villain A low or evil person; originally, a peasant.

voice A vote; consent; approval.

vouchsafe To confide or grant.

vulgar Common.

want To lack.

weeds Clothing.

what ho "Hello, there!"

wherefore Why.

wit Intelligence; sanity.

withal Moreover; nevertheless.

without Outside.

would Wish.

SUGGESTED ESSAY TOPICS

1. Discuss the ways in which the long-standing feud between the Montagues and Capulets helps bring about the tragedy of Romeo and Juliet.

2. How does the concept of masculine honor help bring about the deaths of both Mercutio and Tybalt?

3. Shakespeare portrays Romeo as an adolescent boy. Imagine the play staged in a modern setting. According to his actions, how old do you think Romeo should be and why? Would he act differently today? Why?

4. Do you think Juliet's father really loved her, or did he regard her mainly as a source of wealth and prestige for his family? Explain your answer

5. Show instances throughout the play that indicate Juliet's growing maturity.

TEST YOUR MEMORY

1. Where is the play set?
a) France b) England c) Italy d) Scotland

2. Romeo and Juliet belongs in which category of Shakespeare's works?
a) histories b) sonnets c) comedies d) tragedies

3. Who introduces the play in the prologue of Act 1?
a) Romeo b) the Chorus c) Queen Mab d) Juliet

4. What word or phrase is often used throughout the play to describe the lovers?
a) melancholy b) devious c) star-crossed d) untrustworthy

5. A sonnet, such as the one that opens the play, has how many lines?
a) 14 b) 6 c) 8 d) 12

6. Romeo is part of which family?
a) Capulet b) Montague c) Mantua d) Verona

7. As the play opens, Romeo is in love with which beautiful lady?
a) Rosaline b) Juliet c) Mercutio's sister d) Tybalt's mother

8. How old is Juliet?
a) 21 b) 17 c) 16 d) 13

9. Juliet's parents want her to marry which man?
a) Paris b) Escalus c) Tybalt d) Romeo

10. Where does Romeo first see Juliet?
a) at Friar Lawrence's b) at Capulet's feast
c) at Mercutio's d) on a street in Verona

11. Why does Friar Lawrence agree to marry Romeo and Juliet?
a) He is angry with Romeo's father
b) He is angry with Juliet's father
c) The bishop orders him to do so
d) He thinks their marriage might end the feud

12. After his marriage to Juliet, Romeo becomes related to what man?
a) Capulet b) Mercutio c) Tybalt d) Peter

13. Who kills Mercutio?
a) Romeo b) Benvolio c) Capulet d) Tybalt

14. Who discovers the supposedly dead body of Juliet in her chamber?
a) Lady Capulet b) Capulet c) Romeo d) The Nurse

15. Whom does Romeo kill before he dies?
a) Paris b) Capulet c) Juliet d) Sampson

16. How does Romeo commit suicide?
  a) with his dagger b) with a gun
  c) with poison d) by hanging himself

17. How does Juliet die?
  a) She swallows poison
  b) She jumps off a cliff
  c) She stabs herself with Romeo's dagger
  d) She stabs herself with her father's dagger

18. The action of the play takes place over how many days?
  a) 3 b) 4 c) 7 d) 9

19. How does Lady Montague react to Romeo's banishment?
  a) She dies of grief b) She leaves Verona to be with him
  c) She is happy d) She divorces her husband

20. Who speaks the last words in the play?
  a) Romeo b) Juliet c) Capulet d) Escalus

Answer Key

1. c; 2. d; 3. b; 4. c; 5. a; 6. b; 7. a; 8. d; 9. a; 10. b;
11. d; 12. c; 13. d; 14. d; 15. a; 16. c; 17. c; 18. b; 19. a; 20. d

FURTHER INFORMATION

Books

Evans, G. Blakemore, ed. *Romeo and Juliet: The New Cambridge Shakespeare*. New York: Cambridge University Press, 2003.

Folger Shakespeare Library: Romeo and Juliet. New York: Washington Square Press, 2004.

Manga Shakespeare: Romeo and Juliet. New York: Harry N. Abrams/Amulet, 2007.

Rosen, Michael. *Shakespeare: His Work and World*. Cambridge, MA: Candlewick Press, 2006.

Selfors, Suzanne. *Saving Juliet*. New York: Walker, 2008.

Websites

Absolute Shakespeare
www.absoluteshakespeare.com

Absolute Shakespeare is a resource for the Bard's plays, sonnets, and poems and includes summaries, quotes, films, trivia, and more.

The Official West Side Story Website

www.westsidestory.com

The play and the movie are both featured on this official site for fans, photos, and lyrics.

Play Shakespeare

www.playshakespeare.com

The Ultimate Free Shakespeare Resource features all the play texts with an online glossary, reviews, a discussion forum, and links to festivals worldwide.

Films

Romeo and Juliet (1968) starring Leonard Whiting and Olivia Hussey in the title roles. Called one of the best cinematic versions of the tragedy; narrated by Laurence Olivier.

Romeo + Juliet (1996) starring Leonardo DiCaprio and Claire Danes in the title roles. A 1990s version of the tragic love story, set in Miami.

West Side Story (1961) with Natalie Wood and Richard Beymer. Updating Romeo and Juliet to New York City in the late 1950s, with the feud now between rival gangs; choreography by Jerome Robbins.

Audiobook

Romeo and Juliet. BBC Audiobooks, with Douglas Henshall, Sophie Dahl, and Susannah York, 2006.

Recordings

Prokofiev: Romeo and Juliet. Conducted by Andre Previn. London Symphony Orchestra, 1996.

BIBLIOGRAPHY

Bevington, David, ed. *Bringing Shakespeare Back to Life*. Naperville, IL: Sourcebooks, 2005.

Bloom, Harold, ed. *William Shakespeare The Tragedies: Modern Critical Views*. New York: Chelsea, 1985.

Fallon, Robert Thomas. *A Theatergoer's Guide to Shakespeare's Characters*. Chicago: Dee, 2004.

McLeish, Kenneth. *Shakespeare's Characters*. Studio City, CA: Players Press, 1992.

Shakespeare, William. *Romeo and Juliet*. New York: Houghton Mifflin, 1966.

INDEX

Page numbers in **boldface** are illustrations.

analysis,
of characters, 65–67,
71–72
of scenes, 15, 17, 19–24,
26, 28–31, 33–34, 36,
39–46, 49–50, 52–53,
55–56, 58, 60–61, 64

Benvolio, 15–17, 19, 22, 26, 29,
33–34, 39–40

Chorus, the, 14–15, 28, 76, 79

Elizabeth I, 4, **6**, 7
Elizabethan society, 8–9, 17,
60, 77
and men's roles, 17
and women's roles, 9

fate, 9–10, 14–15, 19, 24, 29,
44–46, 53, 56, 58, 60–61,
65–66, 70, 75–77, 80, 82,
88, 90–91
Friar Lawrence, 31–34, **32**, 36,
38–39, 44–45, 49–50, **51**,
52–58, **55**, 60–61, 63–64,

66–67, 71–72, 77, 79–80,
83–84, 93

interpretation, 87–88,

Juliet, 7–10, 13–14, 17–26, **21**,
25, 28–34, **30**, 36, **37**, 38,
38, 39–47, **43**, **48**, 49–50,
51, 52–58, **55**, **57**, 60–67,
62, 70–80, **74**, 82, 84–88,
90–93

Lady Capulet, 15–16, 20, **21**,
40, 45, 47, 49, 54, 56, 57
Lady Montague, 15–16, 64
language, 26, 79, 82–88, 92
Lord Capulet, 15, 17–19, 25,
40, 45–47, 49, 53, 56–58,
57, 60, 64, 79
Lord Montague, 15–16, 40, 64

Mantua, 44, 49, 52, 58, 60–61,
76
Mercutio, 13, 22–23, 29,
33–34, **35**, 36, 39–42, 60,
66, 73, 76–77, 82, 89, 93
motifs, 78–79
movie and stage interpretations,
89, 92

Nurse, the, 20–21, **21**, 26, 30, 34, **35**, 36, **37**, 42–44, **43**, 47, 49–50, 53–54, 56–58, 66–67, 71–73, 76, 82–83, 87

Paris, 9, 17–21, 45–47, 50, 52–53, 56–58, 62–64, 66–67, 71–74, 79
Peter (Montague servant), 9, 18–19, **18**, 34, 57
poison, 60–61, 63–64, 77, 80, 82
Prince Escalus, 16, 18, 40, 64, 79, 83

Romeo, 7–10, 13–17, 19, 22–26, **25**, 28–31, **30**, **32**, 33–34, 36, 38–47, **38**, **48**, 49–50, 52–54, 56, 58, **59**, 60–67, **62**, 70–80, **74**, 82–93
Rosaline, 17, 19, 24, 26, 28–29, 31, 34, 65, 74, 83, 85, 90

Shakespeare, William, 5
    personal life, 4
sources for *Romeo and Juliet*, 13
symbols, 64, 80, 85, 87–88

themes, 13, 15, 33, 52, 68, 73–77
tone, 92–93
Tybalt, 13, 15, 17, 24–25, **27**, 28, 33–34, 39–42, 45, 47, 50, 52, 54, 63, 65–66, 72, 76, 77, 80, 82, 93

West Side Story, **11**, 69–70, **69**, 92

ABOUT THE AUTHOR

Katie Griffiths is a self-confessed bookaholic who began her love of Shakespeare at an early age. She studied English Literature at University of Edinburgh, where her addictions were further encouraged. She now lives in Hangzhou, China, and teaches English. This is her sixth title for young people. For more information, visit her at katiegriffiths.org